CW00497582

ACKNOWLEDGEMENTS

Some of these poems have previously appeared in the following magazines: *Brando's Hat*, *Dreamcatcher*, *Mslexia*, *Pennine Platform*, *The Slab*, *Staple* and *The Yellow Crane*; as well as in two anthologies *Taste* (ClanU) and *You Can't Make a Hamlet Without Breaking Some Heads* (Blutetouch).

Extracts have been taken from Baudelaire's 'A Hemisphere in her Hair' in the poem 'Sometimes it's Best Not to Read Biographical Details About the Artists you Admire'.

First published in Great Britain in 2006 by Comma Poetry
Comma Press, 3 Vale Bower, Mytholmroyd, West Yorkshire HX7 5EP
www.commapress.co.uk
Distributed by Inpress
www.inpressbooks.co.uk

Copyright © Gaia Holmes 2006

All rights reserved.

The moral right of the author has been asserted.

A CIP catalogue record of this book is available from the British Library

ISBN 0-9548280-8-9

The publisher gratefully acknowledges assistance from the Arts Council England North West, and the Regional Arts Lottery Programme, as well as the support of Literature Northwest, which is itself assisted by ACE NW and CIDS (The Creative Industries Development Service).

Set in Bembo by XL Publishing Services, Tiverton
Printed and Bound in England by SRP Ltd, Exeter

dr james graham's celestial bed

GAIA HOLMES

To Christene and Tallulah

CONTENTS

Suffer me, with great cordiality, and assurance of success, to recommend my celestial, or medico, magnetico, musico, electrical bed which I have constructed... to improve, exalt and invigorate the bodily, and through them, the mental faculties of the human species...

The sublime, the magnificent, and, I may say, the supercelestial dome of the bed, which contains the odoriferous, balmy and ethereal spices, odours and essences, and which is the grand magazine or reservoir of those vivifying and invigorating influences which are exhaled and dispersed by the breathing of the music, and by the attenuating, repelling, and accelerating force of the electrical fire – is very curiously inlaid or wholly covered on the underside with brilliant plates of looking-glass, so disposed as to reflect the various attractive charms of the happy recumbent couple in the most flattering, most agreeable, and most enchanting style.

– Dr James Graham's exhortation to his audience, c. 1763
A Dictionary of Aphrodisiacs, H.E. Wedeck

Constellations

Somewhere
in the middle of a poem
you draw
the shape of the plough
on the stickleback ridges
of my spine.
There is no first line
to explain the beginning.
We start at the centre
and our wicked history
melts away like butter.
Later we walk outside.
The night air
slaps us into sobriety
and you stop me
by the factory
to point out
the constellations
with your artist's finger.
I am not like you.
I don't need
to give everything
a title.
I want to leave this open
and as wide as the sky.
There is no last line
to explain the end.
I want to see the stars
as stars.

Claustrophobia

On the morning bus
I can smell
a hundred lives
in the breath
that crowds the air;
old garlic, weak tea,
cornflakes, porridge.
The man sitting behind me
has the sap
of last night's woman
clinging to his beard,
relics of lust
gunking up the cracks
in his lips.
The office girl opposite
has the almond breath
of forced hunger
and rusty nail-head eyes
that wolf down
the passing hills.
The old woman beside me,
with a scab of jam
on her chin,
smells of raspberries
and loneliness,
I sniff wisps of grief
every time she moves.
There is the stable-scent
of a muesli breakfast
coming from the back,
hot straw and skimmed milk
pushed out by the heat vent.
Someone reeks of guilt,
like violets and sulphur,
like dentists gas
it makes me gag.
This invasion

of sweat, skin, soap
and stale love
is too intimate
for this time of day.
I press myself
against the window,
suck clean coldness
out of glass.

Archaeology

You can burn photographs of faces
but their contours still cling to your skin,
You can define your past as history;
seal it in an envelope marked *Forget*,
but it returns to you as a mantra,
in a certain kind of light, with the scent
of rain-soaked tarmac or the taste of oysters
and his look hits you
with all the force of a fossil
thrown against the soft part of your chest,
his look cuts you as you chop garlic,
his look exhumes every emotion
that you've ever laid to rest.

Seasoned

He said
you have to soak it
in a pint of Bourbon,
leave it over night
so that the reeds drink in
the smoky golden flavours
and soften,
so that when you play
you taste wild fire,
your melodies become
the balmy scent
of Louisiana swamp lands,
the slow smiles
of Mississippi crocodiles,
the creak of moon gazers
on midnight verandas.

I was skint
so I seasoned it
with the corner shop's
bargain lager,
when I played the next day
I made thin symphonies
of cheap neon nights,
girls in frostbite dresses
tottered to my tune,
men in white shirts
roared pitch grass chants
and the devil
at the crossroads
never appeared.

The Burger Man

Out every night from dusk until dawn,
feeding the drunken masses.
He flips burgers in the danger zone
when the streets are streaked
with blood and ketchup.

It's a staggering, swaggering
pumped-up crowd that passes his wagon,
the whole town's on a mission
for a fuck or a fight;
Bambi-legged girls
wearing shoes they can't walk in,
balancing their breasts
like eggs on a shelf.
Men full of seed, shout and bravado
bull-walking to the next bar.

Sometimes they rock the wagon,
plastic sauce bottles waddle like skittles,
hot fat spills, turns the floor
into a greasy rink;
Come on man, gi's a free burger
yu tight bastard
and he locks into the rocking
as a balm,
remembers the slow, calm rhythm
of the Aegean sea,
holds his tongue,
shakes the chips.

In Spring
blossoms fall onto the hotplate,
tremble as they sizzle with onions,
soft perfume seeps into the meat.
He serves his burgers
dressed with petals.

Walking home at night
I know I'm safe
when I see the brightness,
when I smell the bacon,
hear the frying.
Like a grease spattered guardian angel
he reaches through the throb;
Alright darlin', he says.
I'm ok, and you?
I'm fine, he replies
as he wipes salt, ash and mustard
off the counter,
Fine darlin', he says,
always fine.

Clapshot

My mother called it 'Cowboy's Saddle':
that pungent mulch of carrot and swede.
She christened it at a time
when we were spaghetti western bandits
wearing tea-towel bandanas,
galloping around the garden
on our sweeping brush steeds.
It's what the cowboys eat, she said.
It's all the cowboys eat. That and sprouts.

Now at this twisted reunion,
I'm a child being fed by my father
who still scolds me for using too much salt,
who still keeps his love locked in his fists,
whose eyes have become colder and bluer,
whittled by the sharp Alaskan breeze.
Mum used to call this 'Cowboy's Saddle'
I say as I fork up a mound of orange mash.
CLAPSHOT, he says, *Up here we call it 'Clapshot.'*

Wanderlust

All day his fingers hiss
over the old world atlas.
In the evening
he scratches islands
across her back,
etches his restlessness
onto her skin
but tells her
that she is his world
as the welts
start to purple
around the cluster
of mainlands
at the base of her spine.
In her dreams
she lets him go:
papers her walls
with his postcards,
tastes paradise
on a weekly basis,
licks his saliva
off the backs of the stamps.

Living with a Genius

My dog doesn't take drugs.
He can get high on the scent
of March tulips,
levitate above the park
pissing from the heavens
and trailing his toes
over the heads
of Greek gods.

He can read messages
in the wet maps
that stain the pavements,
check the weather on a lamppost,
scan the news on the leg of a bench.

My dog knows
how to chase a ball,
skin a rabbit, catch a stick,
grout the tiles,
remove butter stains
from delicate fabrics,
spell his name backwards,
say 'Thank you'
in 36 different languages
and change engine oil
without spilling a drop.

My dog reads Heidegger
and Wittgenstein
when I go to work,
studies cryogenics and metaphysics,
corrects my poems with red biro,
underlines punctuation errors,
suggests better line breaks.

My dog can catch ghosts,
snap the spines of evil spirits
and scare away burglars
with his intellectual wit.

Voltage

This electric convention
numbs me.
We could light up
the whole city,
twist the neons
around our fingertips
and make the stars obey
like guilty dogs.

The static of our passion
infuses us,
and you sit by the cooker
glowing
like a high voltage saint,
illuminating
the wilderness
I have neglected.

Mr Alhasana

On receiving a business card from an African spiritual advisor

Mr Alhasana says he'll fix it
unpick her name from your heart
and put mine there instead,
embroidered in angel-hair thread.

He tells me to gargle each morning
with limestone and grit,
chant your name as I comb my hair
to the left,
remember the taste of your touch
in my first five waking breaths,
remember the texture of your skin
as I count each dog-tooth bead
on the string he gave me.

Mr Alhasana says he'll bring you back.
I give him the memory of your body
wrapped in our sheets.
He sets them alight and whispers his creed
with a voice that is the dry wheeze
of a sirocco wind.
His words scorch the walls,
your shape appears in burning cotton
and you walk towards me
with your heart on fire.

Planting Paradise

You come home, pockets rattling with seeds:
dry gifts for me to plant in the yard.
You want to nurture pots of paradise.
You want a rich masala of colour
on this flavourless street;
olive trees, mangoes and pomegranates,
chandeliers of fruit glinting amongst
the rowdy tangle of rosebay willow herb.
But bitter soil suffocates the brittle husks
and nothing grows except the weeds.
Dandelions rage, their grey spores drift in
and choke the house with fur.
You stay until the greyness stains you,
until the sun you smuggled fades
then you go away again
to gather seeds, kernels of hope,
bring back your good intentions
swaddled in Indian silk.

Milk

Dawn brings the first trembling roar and rumble of juggernauts.
There is no birdsong thickening with the light,
only traffic – the hiss of wheels and rain like an alibi.
Sunlight shines on the bright molehill of her clothes,
radiates the redness of the dress she never dared to wear.

Laying there she is sodden with the tragedy
of the milkman leaving milk outside his door,
his hand stretching out into the frost, picking up
the first part of his day, pouring cream into his coffee,
stirring the darkness away.

There are two hundred miles between us.
she thinks; black roads and soft white lines
that she wants to gather up
and wear like bandages.

Bleach

He tries not to remember
his black and embarrassing past,
when he took bleach
to school with him in a flask,
sat in the park at lunchtime
slowly burning himself away.

Postcard

I will tell you
of the long, pale nights
and the lullaby of Curlews,
the sweet and salty winds
of Hoy and Papa Stronsay.

I will tell you
of the lime and peacock light
of the Aurora Borealis,
the early whispers of tide
tickling the gravel.

I will tell you
of the soft floss of Sea-thrift
blushing in the shingle
and the Rosa Rugosa
that frames the roads.

I will not tell you
of the rotting seals that reek
in the first breeze of dawn,
the sour gales that pucker
the skin of the Isle.

I will not tell you
of the grey deadpan days
when the Redshanks
shriek their warning
and black magic
licks the shoreline.

I will not tell you
of my fear of stirring the tea
the wrong way,
my fear as I lay awake
feeling the rank mill dam
creep closer and closer.

I will not tell you
that I miss you.
I want to come home
and this North Sea brine
is rusting my heart.

The Performance

Spring pummels the remains
of winter's crust.
Scarlet buds
rocket through the soil
and I grey the day
with facts.

We did not come here
for God as a witness.
We came here
for the pink spume
of cherry blossoms,
the glossolalia
of starlings in the spire
and the scent
of faith soaked stone.

You try to defy
the new green sap in your veins
and play the red devil,
tap dancing and tempting me
from your gravestone stage
as a rusty organ melody
bleeds through
the stained glass body
of Adam.

Smuggling

All day I scan the golden seams of ruins,
scratch my palms over the brusque topography of black volcanic rock.
I take my meals alone, dig fingernails into my phrase book,
try to learn the words for small courtesies and flowers,
try to drown my loneliness in the island's burning sap.

There is a man who only comes with the moonlight,
a man who counts, and quells, each of my anxieties,
a man who brings warm bread and stars to my terrace table
wrapped in a serviette.

And I want to smuggle his love across the Bay of Biscay,
folded in the waxy papers of a perfumed hotel soap.
I want to smuggle the Mediterranean light across the ocean
packed in jars of oil like cubes of Feta cheese.

The Alchemist

Curved over the wheel
chunks of clay changed
to delicate brown lilies
and grew out of the coil
of his hands,
blunt fingers coaxed
stalks into vases.
Bowls went into the kiln
coated in coarse white paste
and came out glowing,
he left them crackling
and cooling on the lawn.
In the morning
they had turned into jewels,
gleaming like beetles
against the shaved grass.

He was always pale
and ghosted with clay,
smelling of wood smoke
and porcelain,
beads of white china
hardened and hung like pearls
in his ginger beard.

Sometimes I'd play
whilst he spun and moulded,
make earthenware cakes,
slice them like fudge
with the cheese wire
and when I'd finished
he'd shape his hands
into a bowl,
I'd rinse my fists
until water turned to milk
and dripped through his fingers.

At Christmas his gifts come to me
packed in gold curls of sawdust,
wisps of Raku smoke
cling to dishes
glazed with ox-blood-red
and lapis lazuli.
And as the urban breeze
stalks and rattles my street,
his wheel hums and whirrs
over the roar of Shapinsay winds.
He baptises fire
with brine.

Living with a Poet

He can find poetry
in polo mints
and parking tickets.
He can coax sonnets
out of bin-bags,
haikus out of fish and chips,
catch moonbeams
in a bread bap,
find the garden of Eden
in the kitchen sink.
He can turn the news headlines
into rhyming couplets,
tame stray dogs
with the hypnotic diction
of his tongue.

When we make love
he comes quatrains
and quintets,
he cums frangipani,
he cums night-scented-stock,
he cums Absinth and aniseed,
Eve's laugh
and Adam's heartbeat,
he cums milk, honey
and manna bread,
he cums sap,
spun sugar and gold dust,
Sometimes I wish
he'd just cum cum.

All day
the heat of his eyes
warms my skin
like fire flies.
He translates my body
into graceful text,

transforms my neck
into Christ's left shin bone,
turns my lips
into an Aphrodite pout,
but this muse's status
is dangerous,
this muse's status
goes to my head.
I broke three toes
and a clavicle
trying to glide
to the corner shop
on the back-draft
of a seraph's wing.

Night

The bedroom window is open.
The coldness of the coming storm
masks the thick scent
of last night's love.
The moon is low
and I am thin as tracing paper,
nothing left but my outline.
My head is full of voodoo,
my frail breath,
like bitter oranges,
and you lie on the bed
in your crucifixion pose.
My task is to keep you alive
with the voltage
of my yew tipped fingers,
to make you cry like the new born.
The dome of the mosque
glints at me across the rooftops
like a fat and mystic eye.
Outside, children crazy on the electric
dance in a trance,
heels thumping, hair streaming,
plastic sandals flapping on warm tarmac.
Tonight the world is full of sprites.

Beans
'St. Jerome forbade nuns to partake of beans because they were
supposedly a strong stimulant.'
(*A Dictionary of Aphrodisiacs*, H.E. Wedeck)

They say there are demons
curled into each tight white bean.
When you eat them
they start making mischief inside you,
sending messages of lust to your brain
so that you want to rub wet silk
against your forehead,
you want to dig your nails
into rotten wood
and flake it like cooked fish,
you want to sing slack, unholy songs
as you scrub the vestry.

In the market
I dip my hand into a vat
and let cold ovals
click through my fingers.
I shake them like wish-bones
in my fist, stuff a palm's clutch
down my smock so that later
I will feel their witchery unfolding.
I will ping my fork against my plate
and pucker the reverence of grace.
I will furrow my nose through the mulch
as I tend the garden.
I will climb up
and lick the stained glass windows,
taste the true colours of sin.

Mr Shark

On receiving a business card from a voodoo practitioner

One phone call from Mr Shark and you'll be
wading through the city traffic like a zombie,
slaloming between taxis, bouncing off buses,
feeling a gravitational pull towards my bed.

When you undress strange relics
will fall out of your pockets:
blood-starched feathers, milk teeth,
my tonsils, rank test tubes
full of mouldy tears and your first
gelatinous confession.

Afterwards, will you remember
each moment of bare skin and unbuttoning
in glorious panoptic detail or will it be
a dark hung-over ache, a mash
of bones, strokes and whisperings
all gummed together with wet dreams
and ectoplasmic sweat?

And what if something goes wrong?
What if a cock crows too early
or a cat shrieks in the wrong register??
Will you suddenly snap out of it
and scowl at me, the dust, the dead moths
and the wine bottles, shake your head
like a dog with a flea in its ear and trot
back to her and her matching cutlery,
her pert cushions, her crisply lacquered nails?

I'm considering contacting Mr Shark
but I think I'll probably let that corpse lie
where it's most comfortable,
beneath her spotless table
looking up at her immaculate legs.

Desert Island Discs

Downing coffee like whisky at a funeral wake,
me, the dog and *Desert Island Discs*.
I'm marooned at this sixteen-acre table
eating toast that fills my mouth
with the whole of the Sahara,
remembering the legend of breakfast in bed.

Passion is a bright parrot you occasionally pull out.
Me – I'm a slave to the cause,
a constellation thief,
throat ripped to fuck from swallowing stars,
dying to shine like Venus, like Pluto, like Mars,
like the big bright planet that I'm not.

I want a light show every morning,
a gala in the yard,
fat cherubs blessing each corner of our bed,
a rain of petals blushing on the skylight.
I want your commitments sculpted out of cumulus
and written in the sky.
I want a sonnet of your devotions
tattooed onto my spine in gold leaf.

Maybe I'm asking too much.

The Basement

Sometimes the librarians
have to go
down to the basement.
They are usually gone
for a while,
return cobwebbed,
panting and blushing,
dust on their noses
and their mouths full
of dangerous words.

The books they bring up
are wrapped
in clueless Hessian,
or bound in Huckaback,
stained with drool
and finger-grease,
warp-paged,
stinking of fish,
and jaggery.

These leprous books
moan and writhe
in the basement
leaking jism and murder.
All day they mutter
cock, cunt, fuck, prick
they whisper lechery,
sing susurrus seduction songs,
hoping to be chosen,
craving the punch
of the stamp,
a new layer of wet dates
on their fly leaves,
dreaming of the hands
that will part their pages
and let their language breathe.

Dead Dog Histories

We are the ones who sit on the sea-board
raw eyed and ogling other people's dogs,
reclaiming salt soaked fur, encasing soft bodies
in our own favourite words.
We are the ones that wear grubby collars
around our necks hidden beneath tartan scarves
or rusted name-tags strung onto chamois threads
pressed into the hollows of our throats.
We are the ones whose houses are full
of bones and ghosts and broken tennis balls.
We are the ones who look off balance, lop-sided,
tugged by invisible spirits as we walk.

Carne

The wheels screech a death rattle
on the Spanish road.
There are gaudy billboards
wedged into the mountains:
matadors hold red flags
like open wounds,
the corporeal sunset
drips over the crusty horizon
and poppies are scabs
on the dry hard shoulder.

Remember this without blood.
Forget the ice packed vows,
the nun-lipped silence,
the long prison sentence
of the tongue,
the captivity of lips
and fingertips,
the deep-frozen laughter.

In the back seat my head hums
with the drone of petrol.
A bag full of meat
reeks and squelches at my feet
and I slip into a rhythmic nightmare
where the sharp eyed waitress
points to her ribs
and says *Carne, carne!!*
where the swarthy men
eye my thighs for a stew,
where you find bones
in my suitcase.

Calypso

A rusty whirly-gig of leaves
scratches the yard,
cats arch and flip
on the witching wind.

There should be crows
marking black smiles in the sky.
There should be red roosters,
Friesian cows and Chagall's blue donkeys.
There should be a symphony of
baying, bleating, scratching, clucking;
a carnival soundtrack to your grin,
a melody to your cooking dance
as you chop, crush and kiss cast iron
with licks of oil and wine.

There should be colours,
an abstract in the kitchen air;
the dark brown of mushrooms,
the black passion of aubergines,
the deep green bite of garlic,
as you skim my spine
with Calypso fingers
and my bones click out
a castanet rhythm.

Living with a Typewriter

Seven o'clock and I'm wearing my best dress
the colour of feathers on a mallard's neck,
legs like liquorice wrapped in black nylon,
hair held up with rosebud pins
and most importantly, painted nails;
a midnight crust that enamels my cuticles
like beetles wings.
They rattle against the letters as I type.

He was waiting at the table when I arrived,
there was no need for small talk,
I unzipped his dust jacket straight away,
pressed my fingers into
the soft dimples of his keys,
ran my thumb across his slick spacebar.
I bought a bottle of Chianti
but he only drinks black ink.
I'm on my third glass of red
and the moon's just nosed
its way through the clouds
to wobble above the rooftops
like a wonky drum of Brie.

We're getting on like a house on fire.
The neighbours are banging on the walls
to complain about the noise
as we make
poems.

The Workshop

He whistles a patchy duet
with the radio
as it slips from muffled Schubert,
and scratches into static.

I'm six years old,
making pies for the world,
numb-fingered with clay
cold as coins
laid on the eyes of the dead.

His workshop is my church.
My relics are
tombstone slabs of earthenware,
powdered pigments
of blood and bone
and the sink plugged up
with porcelain,
a font of the holiest milk.

When they carry coffins
past the window,
streaks of funeral scent
invade the air;
wood varnish, boot polish
and Arum lilies mingle
with the smell of baked earth
and the turnip stink
of our Calor Gas stove.

My father sculpts life
from the dead flesh
of river banks,
he moulds leaf skeletons,
shrew's skulls
and pre-historic mud.
He works with his back
to the black procession.

The Hypnotist

All the 2s, 22. 8 and 4, 84. On its own, number 9.
Her voice is soufflé, salmon mousse and lemon sorbet,
made of light, delicious things.
It's like occasional china kept in locked dressers,
like angel-hair spaghetti, Fabergé trinkets, Elysium harps,
tinkling and trickling over the thick hum of the heating .

1 and 9, 19. 7 and 2, 72. On its own, number 3.
'LINE!!!' a brittle old woman leaps out of her chair
and punches the air, 'OVER HERE!'
There's a mass weak moan of disappointment,
sighing, the shuffling of papers, the sipping of lager
and then it continues.

1 and 4, 14. On its own, number 8. All the 6s, 66.
Outside the world has ceased to exist.
The rain may pound. The wind may roar
but in here is safe: cocooned in the throb of heat,
the fug of smoke, the sound of numbers.
Numbers shine in red rows above the caller.
Numbers leap like lucky eggs into her palm.
Numbers curl like fortune fish upon the table.

On its own, number 4. 1 and 3, 13. 5 and 9, 59.
A man sits alone. His pint, untouched, his card, uncrossed,
just dreaming, calming as he listens to the callers' balm,
drowning in the numbers that she lets into the air.
Prizes glitter on a table at the front of the hall:
teddies wrapped in ribbons and cellophane,
Doulton dinner sets, blown glass swans,
porcelain dolls in Victorian dresses.

All the 8s, 88. 6 and 2, 62. 4 and 6, 46.
Mary has forgotten her aching hip.
Bill has stopped worrying about his hollow house,
the dark indentation in the bed,
and the numbers are landing on arms and faces,
hovering there like moths,
the numbers are smoothing hard corners,
the numbers are soothing and lulling and settling,
 the numbers are letting us breathe.

Cleaning at the Steel Works

My palms spark
in a fizz of washroom cleaner.
I'm tasting the full, cold flavours
of the aluminium sink,
dipping my fingers
into the peachy nectar
of liquid soap.

I love the lemon sherbet smell
of multi-surface spray,
the sound of water
slapping the sides of my bucket.
I love the way the pine floor-gel
sings sweetly over the reeking drone
of the urinal.

On the factory floor
they tame grinding dragons
in their gas flame boiler-suits.
They stand in a glitter
of thin steel rinds.
Blue sparks froth from their hands.
Metal shrieks as it softens and throbs
under the core of heat.

At five o'clock
they unpeel their sweaty armour,
wash their hands and leave
slugs of grease, ball bearings,
wax earplugs and greyed plasters
lined up between my polished taps.

Beneath the rose-pink scent
of industrial cleanser,
the breath of the welder
clings to their skin,
silver parings prick their cuticles
and their lips
taste of cordite.

The Cure

If I catch the whooping cough
they'll take me to Aunty Bronagh's for the cure:
her spit and holy water mixed with orange squash.
They'll make me drink it when they've lit the candles
and said their *Hail Mary's* and Bronagh has pressed
Our Lady against my heart. *Down in one* they'll say
and tip the glass against my lips. I'll gag as I smell
smouldering wicks and taste her thick saliva,
traces of ash, gin and a soft mush of Scotch egg crumbs.

I live in fear of the whooping cough.
Each night I kneel beside my bed and pray. I say
the Our Father, 10 Hail Mary's and the Glory Be.
I say *Jesus please don't give me whooping cough*
so that Aunt Bronagh will have to take it away.

If I get a fever they'll take me to old Aggie's for the cure.
She'll prick her finger and soak the blood
into a Holy wafer spread with Damson jam.
They'll make me eat it, force me to chew on biscuit, fruit and flesh.
I live in fear of fever. Each night I kneel beside my bed and pray.
I say the Our Father, 10 Hail Mary's and the Glory Be.
I say *Jesus, please don't let me get a fever*
so that I have to eat old Aggie's blood.

Maggie McKenna has the cure for burns.
She heals with her old Spam tongue.
I saw her cure Amy Murphy when she burnt herself with chip fat.
Maggie got down on her knees and licked the raw leg like a dog:
long licks from ankle to knee cap. I could hear her tongue
rasping against the sizzled skin. I could smell
something like pork scratchings or scorched Sunday roast.

I live in fear of burns. I do not play with matches. I will not boil the kettl
If I burn myself they will take me to Maggie McKenna's for the cure.
Each night I kneel beside my bed and pray. I say
the Our Father, 10 Hail Mary's and the Glory Be.
I say *Jesus, Please don't let me get burnt.*

Glutton

In some way I am like you: tar mouthed,
fingers smouldering with manic Spanish suns,
eyes like burning Jupiters, lips ready to suck.
See the way I embroider gentle words,
turn them into a carnival of sex and death,
the way my breath smells of hot blood
and simmering things, the way I try
to pickle stars in fat jars that steal their light.
This is me – like you, always wanting more.
Alone at night, after drinking the world dry
I lick Solomon's song from the bible,
steep my tongue in the lust, the dates,
the honey. Get drunk on names, desires
and antiquated ink.

Relic

Oh, to be there now in your small, hot room
with your lime stretch-cover chairs and your china dogs,
with your glass eyed monkeys and your square brass clock,
with you; smoking and swooning as the saloon doors squeak
and stallions hack the dirt with their hooves
and John Wayne swaggers across the screen.

These days I use your scent as valium. It makes me feel soft:
like your pink chiffon headscarves and your fawn kid gloves.
You see, I am not myself. Someone stole my spark
and she keeps it like a firefly, trapped in a jar in her hospital room,
but don't worry Nanna. I will catch moths and lick the silver off their
wings,
I will suck honesty out of earth-worms and I will scream so gently
that it sounds like a song, like the cry of a lonely Tom.

You see, I'm feeling quite displaced.
At night the words turn into strings of pearls that try to choke me.
I forget how to talk, I forget how to dream, I forget how to breathe
but I do not forget you. I carry your glaucomatous eye
in my handbag like a lucky blue marble
and it makes me feel safe.

Desires

We keep our desires
in small cast-iron boxes
with impenetrable locks,
carry them with us
wherever we go
and they weigh us down,
make our hearts feel
like toothache.

Sometimes sounds creep
through the metal:
bird song, slow ferns uncurling,
rain on greenhouse glass.
Sometimes
when we're not concentrating
scents slip out
of the miniscule cracks:
crushed orange peel,
fevers and hot summer skin.

Sometimes our desires
are beyond our control,
they make whirlwinds
in their prisons,
rock their boxes,
scream for honey
and fingertips.
We try to ignore them,
blush and start to fidget,
smother them with our coats
and talk about maths.

Sometimes we're cruel,
we fill the bath
and hold them under water
until they stop babbling,
deprive them
of our dreams.

Gutted

Maybe the day they'd seen
the fishermen gutting fish
had changed her,
maybe she'd been aroused
by the sight
of those slippery organs
popped out like bloody pearls
by salt-scuffed fingers,
maybe she'd been transformed
by the memory of soft metal
stiffened into meat.

That night she was hungry
for dark flavours.
They danced the tango
in the slick and empty harbour.
They Tarantella'd
through flaps of silver skin
and toothpick bones.
Back in their room
when she'd followed
his stinking trail of scales to the bed
he nipped her neck with his teeth
and called her his *Belle Butcher.*
It was a name she didn't like.

Role Playing

It's the soundtrack that defines you.
Your stereo drips sluttish sax,
Stripper's bass and the low hum
of electric violins.
Percussion is the hiss and click
of a Zippo, a shadow-breeding flame
that gilds your lapels
and darkens your chin.

Your table is appropriately cluttered
with empty bottles, cigarette stumps
A–Z's and newspaper cuttings.
It's not an office
but you paste the walls
with faces of women
who may have secrets.
You write your questions
in red biro above their eyes.

The way you spire your fingertips
turns me into a victim or a client:
a woman who has come to you
to ask you to crack the code
of her husband's longing,
to answer the riddle
of the strange kid gloves
balled behind Rolos and wrappers
in the glove compartment.

All I want to do
is talk about simple days
but I find myself creating mysteries
just so that you have the pleasure
of marking maps, tapping phones
and trying to work me out.

Brown Sugar

Up the stairwell
there's a stink of bleach,
beef dripping and fag ends.
Slugs of chip-wrap
leave claggy trails of oil.
Cement steps swallow her footfall
and shriek it back in echo.

He's at the top of the tower
sealed behind a fire door.
His eye in the spy hole
is a squinting sapphire.

She's heard about the magic
he can give, the dreams.
The world becomes the colour
of rosé wine, the flats become
pillars of ivory.
She's heard about crystals
turning into syrup,
sweetness straight into the veins,
gold leaf coating
thin blue tracks.

The heart becomes a pomegranate.
Seeds pound, juice beats,
the world loses its teeth
and dissolves on the tongue.

Her stiff pulse ticks.
He taps the cold steel wish.
It noses its way
through skin and flesh
and everything starts to soften.
The empty December sky
creeps in
and ices her body.

The Island Shop

All we have to offer
is the myth of Corn Crakes,
the rusty wreck, the ruins
and the cold harl
that crushes the secrets of bones
back into their sacred holes.

The tourists come in vibrant trickles;
flapping maps,
crackling in their gaudy raincoats,
weighed down with monstrous cameras
trained to steal the simple colours
of our antiquated lives.

They saunter down the skinny aisles
as if they're in a museum;
touching packets of oatcakes,
squeezing loaves of barmbrack,
holding jars of dark island chutney
up to the light with a reverence
reserved for precious artefacts.

In winter, when the sea's too wild
there is nothing new to perfume our days.
Deprived of its exotic cargo
the island stagnates.
Our gossip thickens like porridge.

Caution

You have baked black bread
with the darkest, sweetest,
most desirable spices.
I have lined my walls
with walnut shells
and brittle charms.

I'm paranoid: wear chicken wire
in bed each night,
keep my heart in the cellar
pickling in brandy.
In summer
when the heat frees its scent
the cats get drunk,
lick the mice to sleep
and I feel safe.

Living with my Alter-Ego

She creeps in at night
to alphabetically file
my iniquities.
In a dustless corner
of my dreams
she snaps, clicks
and shuffles papers,
puts my life
into her own stiff order.
She performs an exorcism
to scour ghost lovers
from my head,
insists on making the bed
every morning,
brushing out creases
with her sharp
axe-head palms.
She is bleach
and frown lines,
red knuckled practicality,
she is the constant
honking drone
of the vacuum cleaner,
the woman who carries
pills and plasters
in her sensible shoulder bag.
She will not let me dwell
in realms of fantasy,
makes me bathe
after each lustful thought,
scrubs my dirty fingernails
until they bleed,
hides all the sharp knives
and buries the corkscrew
somewhere
at the bottom
of the garden.

Exposure

It's Sunday morning
and on Netto's car park
hundreds of people
are selling their lives.
They lay them out on old blankets,
they stack them on trestle tables,
they display them in the boots
of their cars.

They hook you with their eyes
as you pass,
as you finger their silk tassels
and their time stained books:
come buy, come buy, come buy
our lovely lives.

The morning air
smells of guilt, regret and memory.
It smells of wilted intensions   — intentions
and wash-worn clothes.
You can buy pubic hairs
embedded in old Avon soaps,
you can buy 1940's lipstick
on the corner of a stamp,
you can buy lime-scale kettles,
burnt out toasters, second-hand tragedies
and salt-caked shoes.

And they hook you with their eyes
as you pass,
as you fondle rusted cake tins
and chipped terracotta pots:
come buy, come buy, come buy
our lovely lives.

For only 50p you can buy
someone else's history.
You can buy dead wives dresses,

dead babies blue bootees.
You can buy their struggles,
their ambitions, their failed fantasies.
She's selling her wedding gown.
He's selling his porn stash.
She's selling her diet books.
He's selling his hamster cage.

And they hook you with their eyes
as you pass,
as you test zips, rub frays
and button tarnished metal,
as you rummage through skin dust,
death and broken love:
come buy, come buy, come buy
our lovely lives.

A Homesick Truckie in the Algarve Dreams of Bacon

The sun bares its golden chest,
makes the palm trees flirt and sizzle.
Green sap simmers, resin fizzes
and he dreams of bacon.

Days basting on the silver sands
and he's transformed, his lardy pallor
turns from raw prawn to copper god,
his eyes shine with the sweetness
of mangoes, sienna skinned women
wink with their hips, click castanet lips
and he dreams of bacon.

The sunsets are the colour of Sangria.
The petrol demons leave his lungs,
he breathes tangy ocean air,
feels the brine scour his veins
and he dreams of bacon.

He dreams of bacon;
squidged between white bread
so soft and moist it holds
his fingerprints like a plaster cast,
bacon, drenched in a pornography
of lewd ketchup and yellow fat.

He dreams of eating
crispy, streaky bacon butties
in Anne's Motorway Café
as he watches the juggernauts
waddle by and fade into
a grim backlash of sour British rain.

The Summit

My body remembers
each moist syllable
your mouth wrote.
I replay the words
as I clamber up to
the burnt cusp of sleep.
I have no flag of triumph
to plant in the pink peak
of a breast.
I have no tent to pitch
in the cold valleys
of my belly.
I eat Kendle mint cake
like it's bread,
munch slices spread
with a marmite of soil.
In my dreams I'm white fish
frozen in a six foot ice-cube,
dressed in some pink frock
like a cocktail trick,
waiting for your ripe lips
to suck back to flesh
and find me
curled on your tongue,
warm and salty
as a prawn.

The Sugar Demons

In childhood my nightmares
were of the sugar demons.
They'd creep onto my bed as I slept,
fix my mouth open with a stick of Blackpool rock
and wriggle my teeth until they fell out.

My dad wouldn't allow sugar in the house.
We were banned from the sting
of sherbet and popping candy,
banned from midget gems and magic fruits.

He told us horror stories of Aunty Nelly
who could only eat porridge
and mushroom soup,
because the sugar demons had taken
all her teeth.
He told us of DEATH BY TOOTH DECAY,
explained how the poisonous rot
could creep into your blood
and turn it black.

I collected sweet wrappers from the street
and pressed them in a book beneath my mattress,
before I slept I'd scuff my nose
over purple foil and inhale
the ghost scent of chocolate.

Me and my brother saved up
and bought a 1lb bag of Tate and Lyle,
smuggled soup-spoon measures
onto our morning cornflakes,
watched it settle like frost
on autumn leaves and went to school
holding the sweet secret
under our tongues,
nestled like diamonds
in the crooks of our lips.

Sugar's disgusting, my dad would say,
It rots your teeth!
Sugar was a dirty word.
We'd hide in the garden and scratch
the five forbidden letters
into the soil with raspberry canes.
We'd hiss a rustling mantra:
Sugar, sugar, sugar, sugar,
and feel the demon's force
fizzing through our veins.

Religious Education

Each night before we fucked
I'd rub his feet with lavender,
brush the cobwebs off his skin,
pick the spiders out of his hair,
kiss him like a wasp-sting,
shock him into loving.

It was a prelude to the lesson
when he'd melt me
with *The Song of Solomon*,
douse me with honey
and the brown sap of figs,
when he'd pin me down so kindly,
spread my hair across an open bible.

He was subtle,
whispered grace into his lettuce,
kept a vial of Holy water
with the dusters beneath the sink,
mixed God into my morning coffee
but wouldn't have apples
in the house.

Chef

Hard to think of anything
when he's zooming around the kitchen
like a Sahara whirlwind,
when he's having to play octopus
with eight different dishes
and incompetent assistants
who barely know
how to boil a fucking egg.
You have to be steel in this job,
stainless steel,
let the days leave no marks.
You have to be as rough as rock salt,
fiery as Tabasco,
coarse as black-pepper
but his heart melts a little
when he thinks of her crying
because he's shouted at her
for scorching the crème brûlée
again,
he remembers her face puckering
and that perfect lobster blush
swelling her cheeks
and he thinks of her as he plucks chicken,
thinks of her white skin
and her goose pimpled elbows,
he thinks of her
as he kneads the Focaccia,
rubs in oil, pummels,
shapes the dough,
and that makes the day
a little better,
that makes the custard sweet.

Lecture Notes

Today we will be discussing Paul Auster's novel CITY OF GLASS
and its role as both a post-modern and Anti detective novel.
Outside the day is as grey as the nubs of old chewing gum
fossilized to the underbelly of almost every table.
The diggers roar and shriek and grind their way through crusts of tarmac,
clearing the way for more bland blocks, and I dream of mythic
universities;
the ones that smelt of wood and lavender polish. The ones with long
halls
and sweet, dog-eared lecturers with a passion for tweed jackets,
malt whisky and the occasional cigar; the ones with grounds
crowded with honeysuckle and rose-woven architraves,
where students read with their backs pressed against oak trees,
got high on poetry and the thick, spicy scent of knowledge.

Note the allusions to Edgar Allen Poe on page 72,
Note the fractured, frustrating closure of the novel,
Note the way the plot unfolds in static dynamics.
The lecturer is dark and beautiful. Her foreign tongue
turns bland words into delicacies but she speaks too fast,
grins, laughs, gesticulates wildly and I can't concentrate
on what she's saying. All I can think about is whether her curls
smell of coconuts, whether she dabs Vetivert onto her wrists
before she comes to work, whether she drinks her coffee black.

It is a novel that confuses your expectations. Its protagonist
is not a hard-boiled detective. The text is peppered with red herrings.
The girl beside me has drawn an exact replica of Botticelli's Venus
in the margin of her page. Now she is filling it in
with pink and lime green highlighter pens.
Nicola is droning on about buses whilst Gemma sketches bunny rabbits
with a flashing pen topped with purple marabou.
The lecturer is almost dancing now. *Do you all understand??*
Everyone nods vigorously but no one does. No one understands
Freud's theory of THE UNCANNY. No one understands that
words can be like liquid, words can dance, words can eat themselves.

Fear has an object, whereas dread has nothing.
Note the allusions to The Tower Of Babel. Consider the issues
of fate and chance, the mapping of the city, the mapping of the body.
I, myself, am doodling. I am drawing barbs, whorls of spikes
and question marks. I am drawing flying fish.
The girl in front of me is texting beneath the table. A phone,
with a James Bond ring tone, goes off at the back of the class.
Gemma is now carefully applying pastel kitten stickers
 to the lid of her lilac pencil tin. *Do you understand??* I nod.
Everything is questioned. The word becomes the word.
I am dreaming of a dark French café where I drink warm brandy
and knowledge is served to me on a plate with
a hard-boiled detective, two red herrings and a wedge of waxy Brie.

Easter Sunday, Silves

I awake
into a soft bloodshot dawn
taste the battered iron
of Easter bells

outside the sun scratches
like sandpaper
chocolate rabbits wilt
in their gold foil skins

there's a murder
of crushed flowers
on the cobbles
a vivid pulp
on the humps of stone

on dusty pavements
lolling in slices of shade
dreaming dogs twitch and dance
to the drone of the Angelus.

West Central Halifax

Forget the police helicopters
skimming the roof,
churning midnight's tranquillity.
Forget the clusters of wolves
on street corners
that gobble down your legs,
your breasts, your dignity,
and spit them out
pickled with hate.
Forget the syringes
sneering amongst tulips,
the rash of graffiti under the flyover,
the scabs of burnt out cars
on the roadside.

Remember mint flaring:
a sweet green furnace in the yard,
the ripe honky-tonk tune
of the ice-cream van
and the kids running towards it,
brightening the street
with flashes of Indian silk.
Remember the mangoes
in their thick rainbow boxes
stacked outside the cash and carry:
plump orange pods swaddled in tissue
and gold Christmas ribbon.
Remember the song of the Muezzin
carried through the window
on a breeze of spice.

Get Rid of your Problems Tomorrow, you'll Bless the Day you Did

On receiving a business card from an Indian soul reader

She has travelled many regions
to find cures to heal the sick,
shuffled through customs smelling of bark
with her bags packed full of roots
and powdered bone.
If you are weak and can't go on
Suema will make you strong again.
She can remove and destroy bad luck and envy,
she can make your barren womb fruitful.

Standing behind her in the queue at Asda
as she buys her Tetley's tea and her custard creams
you couldn't tell that Suema has dedicated
her life to bring help to the world
unless you sniffed her wrist and inhaled
the mystical aroma of her patchouli basted bracelet,
unless you buried your nose into her hair
and smelt the loitering smoke of the smudge sticks
that make her cat, and some of her clients, vomit.

Her voice is guttural and moist
like clay being gouged from a river bank,
shreds of sage live beneath her fingernails
and she never leaves the house
without her Vesuvius prayer beads
which she clicks whenever rowdy teenagers
sit behind her on the bus.

For only £20 she can stop your family
from turning against you,
she can read your soul, advise you
which meats to eat to make your blood strong,
to keep your husband faithful
she can name the horse that will win
and you can trust her. Suema is confidential,
what you say to her in her room stuffed
with carved ebony and tasselled cushions
will go no further than her friend Rasia.

Six months ago I came to Suema looking for love.
She told me to eradicate yeast and red meat from my diet
and sure enough, after 2 weeks of rice cakes and tinned tuna
I found you, which is why I'm here now
and she's soaping her fingers with lava,
gouging tiger balm into my temples
and telling me that I can save our flailing desire
by switching to decaffeinated coffee
and rubbing a paste of ground capsicum,
wild mustard and honey
into your penis as you sleep
but I think it's a bit too late for that.

On Being Asked to Write an Academic Essay

SYNECDOCHE PERJORATIVE EPITHET
METONYMY TRAJECTORY JUXTAPOSITION
All day these words creep into my throat
like paracetamol,
these words – like prescription drugs
that should be handed over the counter
in plain white bags,
left in the medicine cabinet
next to fossilised Lemsip
and Milk of Magnesia.

These words don't fit into my mouth.
They are multi-complex shopping centres
bulging out of my cheeks.
They are sour grapes mixed with salt,
kipper bones, surgical and sharp
making small, neat incisions in my brain
as I try to sleep.

These words aren't mine.
I lift them out of their wrappers
with tweezers
and lay them on the page
where they stare at me for hours,
unblinking,
dead fish on a gutting slab.
My own words shiver under the table,
timid dogs waiting for my tongue
to take them back
and roll them in the air with relish.

These words are now sleeping
in the same bed as me.
They are cold jointed
and pickaxe limbed.
My own words curl
trembling at my feet,
occasionally try to creep
under the covers,
bring me breakfast in the morning:
steaming mugs of ambrosia
and constellations on toast.

Danger Money

I breathe in a morning cocktail
of birdsong, dew and exhaust fumes,
grit my grin against the wind and rain
and take up my crucifixion pose
in the middle of the road.

Holding my lollypop stick like a trident
I stop minis, Mercedes, juggernauts,
jaguars, buses and ants.
I part a sea of traffic
to let the children cross.

My mouth aches from the strain of smiling,
the 8 o'clock breeze inflates my coat
and I struggle to stay earth-bound;
a tottering lime green balloon
glued to the day
with a flypaper stretch of tarmac.

Hollow

She gulps down risk
like aspirin.
Numb headed and delirious
on thirty five quid lust,
she'll break her back
for a meaningful fuck,
wear her angel suit
until they dim the lights
and she sweats opium,
shrieks like a calving whale.

She's the girl
with the heaven-dust hair,
the surgically enhanced wings.
She's the girl
who likes to stick her tongue
into the world's honey,
who likes to suck and suck
until she's so sweet
she makes them sick.

She's the girl
who frames up
lecherous looks
like butterflies,
to remind herself
that some meaning
rested on her
for more than
twenty seconds.

Sometimes it's Best Not to Read Biographical Details About the Artists you Admire

Today Baudelaire fell off his pedestal:
keeled over like a condemned tower block,
cracked his head on the corner of the gas fire.
Today I didn't bother to refill his glass
and got mildly annoyed by
yet another Absinthe stain on the carpet.
He lay there flapping his gawky ruffled wrists
waiting for me to notice: *It's time to get drunk*
he squeaked *We must always be drunk*
but today I didn't dig it.

Today his sweet aniseed breath
made my stomach spin.
The pompous angle
of his crushed silk cravat
annoyed me, intensely.
He tried his old charm tactics:
In your hair's glowing hearth
I breathe the fragrance of tobacco
blended with opium and sugar
I turned the radio on.
Spun the volume dial up to 10.

In your hair's dawning shores
I am exalted by the confused aromas
of tar and musk and coconut oil.
I said nothing – went upstairs to pack his things.
I stuffed his blackness, his delusions,
his vast collection of pornographic videos,
his S&M whips, studs and hot pants,
his toxic green vices and his
syphilis soaked notebooks into a bin bag
then I opened the curtains
and let in the light.

Resourceful

It's the way we were brought up.
We reclaimed histories,
prospected for gold
in wild roots and clover tips,
re-boiled slips of soap
in a cast-iron pan
to make brand new lumpy bars.

After dark we took family outings
to the local land-fill site,
smelt the evenings' cold frosts
mixed with leaked battery fluid,
wet rugs and soft mahogany.
We'd return with a booty
of Bakelite radios and scratched 45's,
lay rain-warped atlases out to dry.

Those old habits linger.
My mother still brews up
hedgerow tea on midsummer's eve,
my father coaxes shipwrecked beams
into fresh foundations
and I believe
that there are veins of hope
in every broken thing,
there is always life
beneath the choke of rust.

The Nightdress

Just touching it makes her think
of stiff beds and laughing nurses,
pale green sheets
and the squinting doctor who told her;
You is not crazy. You is not a nut.
You is just lonely, you have ze nice legs.
Why has a pretty like you no husband?
you must smile more and be happy,
ze nice legs will be happy,
then the love will come.
Then you will be good.'
The diagnosis brought her a lover
with a long, white, breakable neck,
mad as a dog drunk on the wind,
mad as a bus going backwards.
Mad but beautiful.
As beautiful as the silence
she has learnt to coat her walls with.
Beautiful but dangerous.
She tries not to let him hear her
whispering prayers.

It

It made her want to drink the last of the Christmas sherry,
climb over the park railings after midnight,
and cry at Adonis's marble feet.

It made him want to phone in sick
and spend the rest of the day in bed with her,
eating treacle sponge and custard, playing chess.

It made them want to go to the next alcoholics anonymous meeting.

It made him want to go to the forest
with a weeks supply of cream crackers, tinned sardines
and his dead grandmother's fat, 3 stone bible.

It made him want to pull out his tubes,
curse at the nurses
and walk to the gardens to smoke a cigarette.

It made them want to adopt.

It made her want to touch his wife's breasts
to see if they were real.

It made them want to drive to the seaside on a rainy day,
park up on the crest of a cliff, eat egg mayonnaise sandwiches,
drink tea from a thermos flask and watch the grey waves
curling and rolling through steamy windows.

It made him want to apologise.
It made her want to murder.

It made her want to wear chiffon dresses
the colour of ostrich steak.

It made him want to go to the library
and borrow a book on goat husbandry.

It made her want to paint all the windows with bitumen,
burn his letters and cry for six weeks.

It made him want to eat fried rice with a pair of tweezers.

It made them want to slow-roast the placenta
in a casserole dish with Bisto, onions and leeks.

It made her want to pour treacle
into the toecaps of all his trainers.

It made him want to teach his Jack Russell how to iron.

It made her want to set fire to her Barbie doll's hair.

It made her want to move to Russia,
gorge on roast turnips and black bread
and become comfortably fat.

It made him want to touch her clavicles.

It made her want to wear a false moustache
at the wedding reception.

It made him want to curl up in a fist
at the bottom of her bed.

It made him want to steal a triangle of Brie
from Sainsbury's deli counter.

It made her want to sell her soul on eBay.

It made her want to try it when her parents were out.
It made him want to think about it for a long time in the bath.
It made them want to forget about it and get on with their lives.

Packing

tomorrow
she will stuff
the essence of her life
into a little orange suitcase
fold up blackness
like an unworn funeral dress
roll slivers of his sweat
into bundles
like small neat sushi
as raw and salty
as the rain
that oils the rooftops
at 2 am

El Dia de los Muertos

He's coming back.
Madre says I must not cry,
Madre says I must not make his path
treacherous with tears.

For days we've shaped and baked
bones dipped in sugar,
death bread crisp as skulls.
I've made my own heart
out of cochineal and marzipan
and I'll lay it on his black bed
with marigolds and figs
split like small organs,
wait for him to rise.

Tonight the living and the dead
will crack ribs and kneecaps,
the street will rattle with
the dry dance of the *calavera*,
the air will smell of hot wax
and angst quelled with tequila,
my jaws will ache as I crunch
through skins of dough,
the almond meat of my heart
will itch for the kiss
of his stale teeth.

Madre says I must not cry,
Madre says
we must guide him back in
with our joy.

And tonight I will laugh.
I will laugh like a monkey
drunk on sour fruit,
I will laugh with my mouth
so wide that I swallow
huge chunks of the night
and I'll roll his soul in candy,
feel his old dust
sweetening my veins.

Voice

Your voice sways the stars,
they move as if they're drunk;
stumbling and swaying through
the dark blue stretch.
You fill these hours
with the scent of grass and soil.
You make me believe
that you will open the sky
and summon cool mists
over the cracked yellow valleys
of my head.

Some of the Nicer Things he Said

He said I was
a fairy tale wilderness
that all the bandits
passed through.

He said I was
a rum-soaked saloon bar
where cowboys spat
and spun their guns.

He said I was
a red bulls-eye target,
a hole in the head
and he's better off dead
without me.

He said I was
a wisp of pink smoke,
a hooker's frothy boa,
a lying rose,
a Venus fly trap.

And he said he was
twitching,
slowly dying
in my sap.

Peninsula

You walk it like a tightrope,
broad feet turned out,
balancing your way
along the skinny peninsula.
This is the penultimate side-show,
your dextrous circus trick.
I'd rather there was this link between us,
this bony joint of sand and grass
than the distance of you
on your dog-eared island
drifting further and further away.
Your letters are rare now.
You send me dislocated objects:
chips of lustre
hacked from oyster clasps,
fat lenses of jellyfish
packed in jigsaws of ice,
fossils that thud through the door
and crack on the white porch tiles
revealing histories
that have nothing to do
with you and me.
And lately you have been sending
razor shells and cuttle bones,
things too sharp for remembrance,
pictures of your house
sinking back into the sea,
your name dissolving
as the ink runs dry.